The Nature Kid's Guide to
CHICKENS

DAVID ANDERSON

LP Media Inc. Publishing
Text copyright © 2026 by LP Media Inc.

For information address LP Media Inc. Publishing,
30012 Variolite St NW, Princeton MN 55371
www.lpmedia.org

Publication Data

Chickens
The Nature Kid's Guide to Chickens — First edition.

Summary: "Learn all about Chickens, the Nature Kid Way"
— Provided by publisher.

ISBN: 979-8-89818-180-2

[1. Chickens – Non-Fiction] I. Title.

Title: The Nature Kid's Guide to Chickens

CONTENTS

COOP LIFE

A chicken can remember the faces of more than 100 other chickens — and they never forget a friend!

Cluck, cluck! A hen struts across the sunny farmyard.

Chickens live in a coop on the farm. A coop is like a small house made just for birds. It keeps them safe from rain, wind, and hungry foxes.

Inside, hens rest on soft nests of straw. At night, chickens sleep on wooden bars called roosts. They grip tight with their toes and never fall off – even in their sleep!

Most coops have a door to a fenced yard. Chickens love to walk around outside and feel the warm sun on their feathers. A good coop is a chicken's castle.

JUNGLE ROOTS

There are more than 33 billion chickens on Earth. That's more than any other bird!

Rustle! A bright wild bird darts through the thick jungle leaves. It's a Junglefowl!

Long ago, chickens did not live on farms. Wild birds called red junglefowl still live in the jungles of Asia today. They look a lot like the roosters you see on farms.

Red junglefowl are shy and quick. They hide in thick brush and tall grass during the day. At night, they fly up into trees to stay safe from tigers and snakes.

People started to tame these wild birds about 8,000 years ago. Over time, they became the farm chickens we know and love. Every chicken alive today has jungle roots!

SMALL BUT MIGHTY

The world's tallest chicken breed, the Malay, stands over two feet tall!

Pip, pip! A little bantam runs into the sun. She's half the size of other chickens!

Chickens come in many sizes. Some are as tall as your knees. Others are small enough to sit in your hands. Most weigh about 5 to 8 pounds.

Tiny breeds are called bantams. A Serama bantam weighs less than a pound! Big breeds like the Jersey Giant can weigh 13 pounds or more.

Even small chickens are strong. They can hop over logs and push through thick weeds with ease. Big or small, every chicken is one tough bird.

COMBS AND CLAWS

Flap! A rooster shakes his bright red comb in the morning sun.

A chicken's body is built for farm life. On top of its head sits a bright red comb. Under its beak hangs a soft flap called a wattle. Both help the bird cool off on hot days by releasing extra body heat.

Strong claws help chickens dig in the dirt for bugs and seeds. A sharp beak lets them pick up tiny morsels. Feathers keep them warm and dry in all kinds of weather.

Each part of a chicken has a job. From comb to claw, this bird is perfectly made for life on the farm.

SUPER SIGHT

Swoop! A sharp-eyed hen spots a hawk above and dashes to safety.

Chickens have amazing eyes. Each eye sits on the side of the head. This lets them see almost all the way around (about 300 degrees) without even turning!

One eye can look up for hawks while the other looks down for food. Each eye works on its own, like two cameras both filming at once.

Chickens also see colors very well. Sharp eyes help them find food and stay safe from sunrise to sunset.

Chickens can see ultraviolet light — colors that human eyes cannot see at all!

FUNKY FEATHERS

Poof! A fluffy Silkie struts by looking like a cotton ball!

Not all chickens look the same. Some have spots. Some have stripes. Others are solid black, white, or gold. The world has over 500 chicken breeds!

Silkie chickens have fluffy feathers that feel like silk. Polish chickens sport a wild puff of feathers on their heads like a fancy hat. Frizzle chickens have curly feathers that stick out in every direction.

Each breed has its own special look.

Silkie chickens have black skin, black bones, and even black meat under their fluffy white feathers!

PECK AND SCRATCH

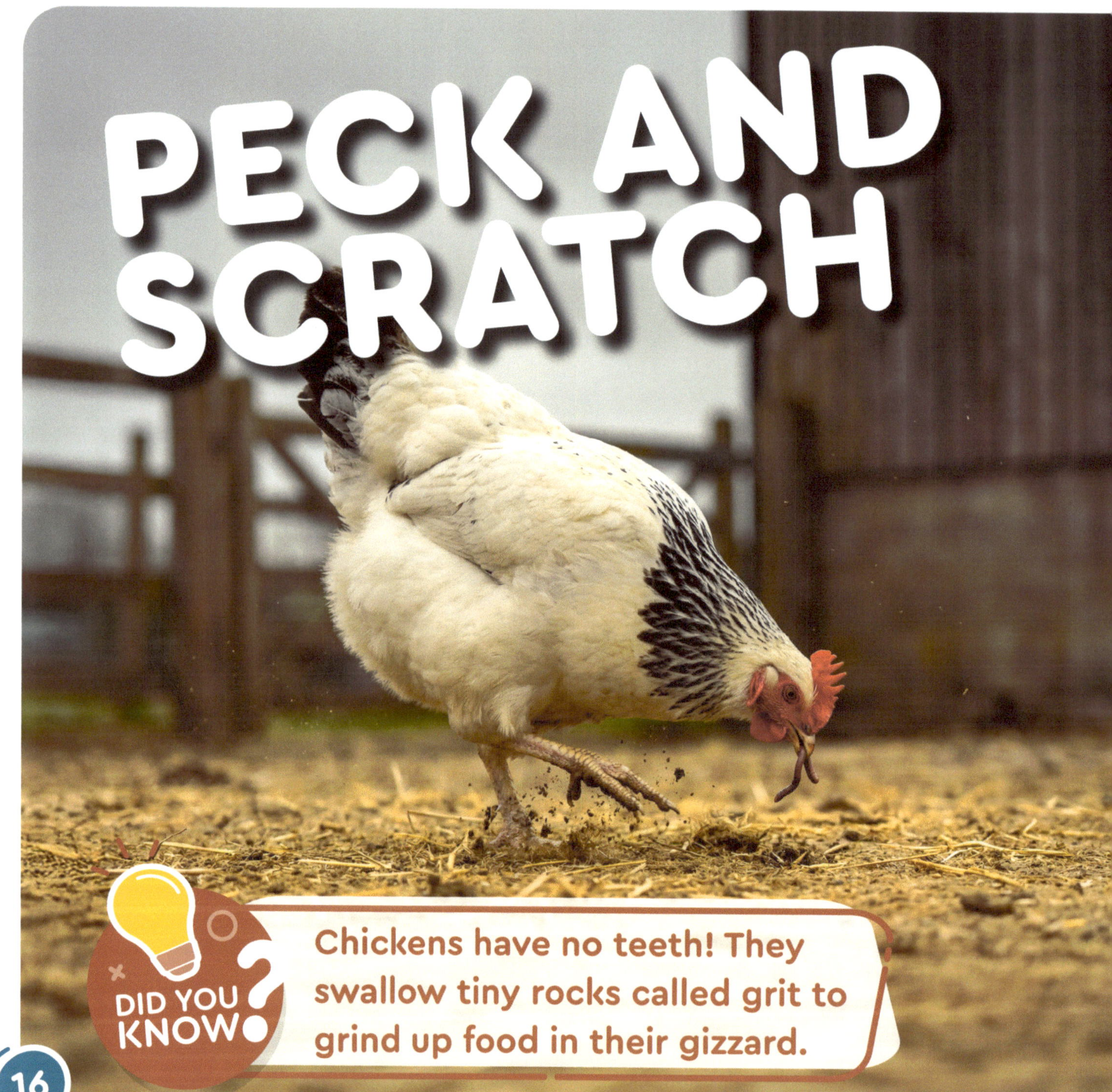

Scratch, scratch! A hen digs up a juicy worm from the dirt.

Chickens are not picky eaters. They munch on seeds, bugs, grass, and fruit. A chicken will peck at almost anything to see if it is food!

To find a meal, a hen scratches the ground with her feet. She kicks up leaves and dirt to find hidden bugs. Then... snap! She grabs it in her beak before it can escape.

Farmers also give chickens corn and grain. They spread it out and let the chickens scratch the ground looking for it. Fresh water is a must, too. A happy chicken is one with a full belly and a cool drink.

EGG TIME

FUN FACT!
Champion laying hens can produce about 300 eggs per year — almost one every single day!

Plop! An egg plops out onto the straw. A chicken sits on it.

Hens lay eggs in quiet, cozy spots. Many hens use nesting boxes filled with straw. Most lay one egg every 1–2 days.

Eggs come in lots of colors! Some are white. Some are brown. A few breeds even lay blue, green, or pink eggs. The color depends on the breed, not what the hen eats.

An egg has a hard shell on the outside. Inside, the yolk gives food to a growing chick.

People enjoy eating eggs for breakfast, lunch, and dinner, too! Last year, over 93 billion eggs were sold in the United States alone!

CLUCK TALK

DID YOU KNOW?
Chickens make over 30 different sounds - including separate alarm calls for ground and sky predators!

Bawk, bawk, bawk! A chatty hen talks to her friends across the yard.

Chickens talk to each other all day long. They use clucks, squawks, and purrs to share how they feel. Each sound has a special meaning.

A loud alarm call means danger is near — one call for hawks, a different one for foxes! A soft cluck tells chicks to come close. Roosters crow to say, 'This is my space!' Hens coo when they feel calm and safe.

Even baby chicks peep before they hatch. They can hear their mother's voice right through the shell. Cluck talk starts before a chick even sees the world!

DAWN PATROL

Roosters have a built-in body clock — they often crow before dawn, sometimes as early as 4 in the morning!

Cock-a-doodle-doo! A rooster crows loud to wake the whole farm up.

Chickens wake up with the sun. As soon as it gets light, they hop off the roost and start their day. Breakfast comes first!

All morning, chickens peck and scratch for food. They take breaks to rest in the shade when it gets hot. In the afternoon, many hens find a cozy spot to lay an egg.

As the sun goes down, chickens head back to the coop. They climb up to their roost and settle in for the night. Lights out — until tomorrow's dawn patrol begins again!

ZOOM AND FLAP
DID YOU KNOW?
A chicken can sprint about 9 miles per hour — fast enough to outrun most people in a short race!
24

Whoosh! A hen zooms across the yard with her wings spread wide.

Chickens may not fly far, but they sure can move! A chicken can run fast on its two strong legs. It dashes and darts to get away from trouble in a flash.

When a chicken needs a boost, it flaps its wings hard. It can fly up to a fence or into a low tree branch. Most flights are short: just a quick hop and flap, then back to earth.

Chickens also use their wings for balance. Watch one turn a sharp corner and you will see its wings pop out to keep it from tipping over!

DUST BATH

DID YOU KNOW?
Chickens love their dust baths so much they sometimes take one for 20 minutes or more!

Whomp! A cloud of dust rises as a hen wiggles into the dry dirt.

Chickens take baths, but not with water! They use dirt instead. A hen digs a shallow hole, then flops in and wiggles around. Dust flies everywhere!

The dirt gets deep into the feathers. It smothers tiny pests like mites and lice. After a good dust bath, a chicken shakes off and fluffs up, clean and happy.

Dust baths are also a way to relax with friends. Chickens often bathe in a group, lying in the warm sun together. It looks like a chicken spa day!

PECKING
ORDER

Brawk! Two hens face off to see who is the boss.

A group of chickens is called a flock. Every flock has a pecking order. It is a ranking from top bird to bottom bird.

Top chickens eat first and get the best roosting spots. Lower birds wait their turn. Chickens work out the order with pushes, pecks, and stare-downs. It can get dramatic!

Once the order is set, life is calm. Most birds know their place and follow the rules. A peaceful flock is a happy flock.

Add a new chicken to a flock and chaos begins, the whole pecking order must be figured out again!

ROOSTER RULES

Thump! A rooster stamps his feet and puffs up to look extra big.

Roosters are male chickens. They are often bigger and louder than hens. A rooster has long, colorful tail feathers and sharp spurs on his legs for protection.

A rooster watches over his flock like a guard. He keeps an eye out for foxes and hawks, sounding the alarm if danger appears. He also finds food and calls the hens over to eat before he takes a bite himself.

A rooster does a special 'tidbit dance' — he bobs his head and drops food to impress a hen!

CUTE CHICKS

DID YOU KNOW?
A chick grows from a tiny dot to a fully formed baby in just 21 days inside the egg!

Crack! A tiny beak pokes through the shell and a wet chick peeks out.

Baby chickens are called chicks. To hatch, a chick uses a small bump on its beak called an egg tooth. It taps and pushes until the shell finally cracks open. This hard work can take a whole day!

A new chick is wet and tired. But in just a few hours, it dries off and becomes a fluffy ball of soft down. Soon it can walk and peck at food.

Chicks are tiny but brave. They follow their mother everywhere and chirp loudly when they are hungry or cold. Within weeks, they start growing real feathers.

HOVER HENS

DID YOU KNOW?
A broody hen turns her eggs up to 50 times each day so every side gets warmed evenly!

Coo! A mother hen calls softly as her chicks huddle under her wings.

A mother hen is called a broody hen. She sits on her eggs to keep them warm. It takes about three weeks. She barely eats or drinks while she waits!

Once the chicks hatch, the mother keeps them close. She fluffs her feathers so they can snuggle under her like a warm blanket. She clucks softly to keep them calm.

The hen also teaches her chicks what to eat. She pecks at the ground to show them how it's done. She never lets her babies out of sight until they are ready to explore on their own.

BUG
BUSTERS
DID YOU KNOW?
Chickens will eat almost anything that moves: including small mice, frogs, and even snakes!

Snap! A hen catches a grasshopper right out of the air in one bite.

Chickens are great bug hunters. Let a few hens loose in a garden and watch them go! They gobble up beetles, slugs, ticks, and ants like feathered vacuum cleaners.

Farmers love this free pest control. Chickens eat bugs that harm crops and plants. No sprays or traps are needed — just hungry hens on the job.

Chickens also eat weed seeds before they can sprout. This helps keep gardens clean and tidy. A flock of hens is like a little clean-up crew that works for food scraps!

FEATHERED FRIENDS

Purr! A gentle hen nestles into a child's arms for a cozy cuddle.

Chickens make wonderful farm friends. Many kids raise chickens as pets. Some hens love to be held and petted, just like a dog or cat!

Chickens get along with other farm animals, too. They walk beside goats, ducks, and even horses without any fuss. A calm chicken can share a yard with all kinds of critters.

Taking care of chickens teaches kids a lot. You learn to be kind, patient, and responsible for another life. A chicken can be a true friend — one that gives you fresh eggs and happy clucks every single day!

GLOSSARY

coop
A small house where chickens live and sleep

roost
A bar or perch where chickens sleep at night

comb
The fleshy red crest on top of a chicken's head

wattle
The soft flap that hangs under a chicken's beak

flock
A group of chickens that live together